SURVIVING

THE STOP

Change the Atmosphere, Change the Outcome

By Retired Senior Special Agent
US Department of Justice

Bobby F. Kimbrough, Jr.

with Mercedes L. Miller

Perfect Publishing

ISBN-13: 978-1-942688-16-7

Printed in the United States of America

DEDICATION

Surviving the Stop is dedicated to all the men and women who protect and serve throughout our nation.

Surviving the Stop pays homage to those men and women who lost their lives or were victims of traffic stops.

Surviving the Stop is in honor of those who lost their lives while protecting and serving.

This book is not about right or wrong: the sole purpose is to educate and prevent future loss of life and property. SURVIVE THE STOP.

ACKNOWLEDGEMENTS

Because of the many people who impacted my life over the years, I could fill up a book expressing my gratitude and extoling my sincere appreciation. Know that every person who has had a hand in my professional development and ascension, your contribution to my existence is valued and acknowledged.

Specifically for Surviving the Stop, I must extend a heartfelt thank you to the brilliant creator of CEO Space International Berny Dorhman and his wife Penelope. The unparalleled support you provide in a remarkable environment has been the spark that lit a forest fire ablaze in my life. Thank you.

For those whose words and efforts specifically inspired me on this project – David Corbin, Dr. June Davidson, Dr. Robert Johnson and Harry Lay – you have no clue the magnitude of your contribution to Surviving the Stop and these great United States of America.

To Bishop Neil Ellis of Global United Fellowship – thank you for opening the door for me to serve and protect men and women of God on an international level. The opportunity you have afforded me and prayers you have extended to me as I work to ensure safety and security in the Kingdom is a blessing to me personally and professionally. To Bishop Sir Walter Mack, my spiritual covering for more than 10 years, the honor to serve you, your family and your ministry is immeasurable. The spiritual wisdom, theological guidance and sound teaching you provided for me is ever embedded in my heart and spirit; I am a stronger man of faith because of our connection.

To my colleagues in the Greensboro Resident Office (past and present), my life would not have been and would not be such a successful journey without you - thank you. Otis — our partnership continues long after the cases are solved, and the guns and badges are shelved; I appreciate you tremendously. To Assistant United States Attorney Sandra Hairston, it has been my great honor over the years to work with you, to learn from you and to support you in your phenomenal work for our great nation. To David Hege, Cedric Russell and the brilliant ones at Grace, Tisdale and Clifton, you are astute business men who have shared your unparalleled knowledge, keen sense of community and overwhelming support throughout the years — you are appreciated.

To my amazing Mother and Father, (Viola and Bobby, Sr.), my incredible family (seven astonishingly, wonderful boys), my confidant and dear friend Mercedes Miller — without you all, none of this would be possible. You have been my stabilizing force and inspiration to dig deeper and go higher.

The ultimate thanks goes to the Author of all life, and most certainly the Author of my life. May God continue to bless me and bless this great nation.

CONTENTS

FOREWORD

Protecting public safety is our nation's top priority. The most important element of that mission is the bond between law enforcement officers and those they serve. I say "bond" because a bond includes a trust, a promise, an oath to serve each other. Experienced officers know that building the bond crucial to safe and healthy communities. We cannot educate, work or worship as we deserve if our neighborhoods are unsafe, and all of us have a responsibility to do our part in that effort.

We demand and expect our law enforcement professionals to train their officers about the diversity that makes our country great. When those officers fail, we can and should hold them accountable. But we must also educate ourselves and our families about the other side of that coin – the pressures and demands that face those officers, and how we can react and respond in a manner that strengthens the bond between us. Surviving the Stop guides us in that direction.

Bobby Kimbrough and I have worked together over a 30 year period in his role as a Winston-Salem police officer and US Federal Agent, and my role as an Assistant District Attorney, United States Attorney and criminal defense lawyer. Bobby is uniquely qualified to offer this guidance to all of us regardless of our age, race or economic status. We all have a part to play in the health and safety of our communities – and we want to do our part. Surviving the Stop makes that possible!

Walter C. Holton, Jr.
United States Attorney
Middle District of North Carolina
1994 to 2001

INTRODUCTION
You Can and Do Have an Impact – Survive

In my 30 years inside of law enforcement, I have seen firsthand the impact of bad choices, flip decisions and spur of the moment actions and how it negatively impacts both sides of the badge. There is without question an undeniable need to understand and be understood as those who exist in our society look to law enforcement for protection and service; at the same time, there is a distinct necessity by law enforcement to be allowed to do their jobs with respect and deference. Surviving the Stop is an effort to bridge the gap between those who serve and protect and those who need to be served and protected. We must realize that the need to co-exist is essential because we are truly connected.

Law enforcement officers of all kinds work in a service industry where they have committed to putting their lives on the line every single day. Every day when they go in to perform their tasks and earn a living, their lives are at risk. And while major, national events illuminate the severity of what can happen in the work-life of law enforcement every day, the light is rarely shone upon the brave acts, fearless feats and precarious problems that officers are required to carry out as a part of their job responsibilities - every - single - day. The traffic stop is one element of the vast array of the life threatening and life changing job responsibilities, thus, the severity and complexity of the expectations must be comprehended. When others are fleeing the problems and premises – law enforcement is going toward it. It is not only unfathomable by many who do not understand all that an officer has to contend with it is continuously unconsidered.

When thinking about what law enforcement officers have to contend with in their everyday work and how it impacts the lives of every citizen in this country, I often reflect back on that day in our country's history that most will never forget. The day when two Boeing 767 Airplanes crashed into the Twin Towers and demolished what we knew as the World Trade Center. I remember the plane that destroyed an entire wing of the Pentagon. Now replay in your mind the footage you saw on television news casts and the images in print media. Take it one step further. Who were the people running toward the mayhem and chaos while others were running away? Who were the people rushing toward the danger and peril? Along with their fellow emergency personnel colleagues, it was those known as New York's Finest who were running into the face of danger. It was law enforcement officers who were risking their lives when all others were working to save their own.

And while we thankfully do not experience events like the September 11th terrorist attacks on a daily basis, there are many types of crisis that require someone to risk their own lives to step in and mitigate the risk to save others. It takes a different type of individual to strap on and step up. It takes a certain type of individual to serve and know they are being viewed under a microscope. The reason they are able to do it is because they have an innate desire to serve and protect. At the core of their being they want to know how they can make a difference.

There are indeed a few undesirables in our distinguished profession. They are the exception and not the rule. Let's just all agree that there are undesirables in every profession. Our country must make a conscious decision to respect those who are honorable and allow them to effectively do their job while holding accountable those who go astray. We can all impact the outcome if we consider our contribution to the atmosphere in this regard.

Law enforcement must also take responsibility and accept that they too can change the atmosphere. Law enforcement, along with carrying the badge, must realize the impact they have upon every person they come into contact with on this career path. Law enforcement must know and embrace the truth that every time they meet someone they leave an indelible footprint, an undeniable impression. Walking, driving, exiting the vehicle, speaking to citizens – everything shapes the view of those they encounter.

One law enforcement professional who does something intentional or unintentional, malicious or not malicious – they have the capacity to impact how others view the profession for the rest of their lives. Having said that - no two professionals are the same. Just as the citizen wants to be treated as an individual on their own merit - so, too, does the officer.

As we embark upon this journey together to ensure you and those you love Survive the Stop, know that my desire is to bridge the gap between the protectors of life and the livers of life in this great nation. The sole purpose of this writing and the conversations that will ensue is to save lives and change the atmosphere that currently exists in our society. If we can change the atmosphere, we can change the outcome.

THE ULTIMATE GOAL – SURVIVE THE STOP

In any encounter with law enforcement, your ultimate goal is to come out alive. Period. This is not a time when you work to match wits, show how smart, tough or strong you are. This is a time when your focus should be on getting home safely and continuing your life with little impact once you and the officer have parted ways. Your ultimate goal is to exit with your life and without bodily harm to you, the officer or anyone else in or around your automobile.

Surviving The Stop

The other key element to consider is that surviving the stop is also about financial damage in several capacities. While your ultimate goal is to get out of the traffic stop alive, you also want to emerge with the least amount of monetary damage as possible. Fines and penalties can become costly in traffic stops. There are specific things you want to be mindful of to avoid fines, penalties, points on your insurance and court costs. Simple actions and reactions can make the difference in whether or not a simple traffic stop escalates from a verbal warning to a written warning to a ticket to an arrest to a court appearance. Too often you have the power and you don't even realize it. Too often you have the power but you forget the ultimate goal – Survive the Stop and come out with the least amount damages for you.

The power you have must be exercised intentionally and with keen awareness. What you do during a traffic stop can affect the rest of your life. Frequently in the heat of the moment you do not take into account the impact your choices will have on your present and on your future. Without question, you are where you are in this place in your life because of each of the choices you have made. You do not have the ability to control what another person will say or do. You do have the opportunity to manage how you act and react in every situation. Because of the positive and negative outcomes that can emerge from a traffic stop, you must make a conscious decision to use your power to Survive the Stop with the ultimate goal in mind.

Change the traffic stop and change your life. All human beings desire to be in a better space and a better place. Each person wants a peaceful and prosperous existence for themselves and their families. While a traffic stop is one particular moment in time, it can have a major impact on your entire life. The inability to manage your emotions in high stress and high pressure situations yields the opposite of what you desire. A sarcastic comment, a snide remark, a disrespectful stance can trigger an undesirable situation which impacts your current state and taints your entire future. A knee-jerk reaction can escalate to disorderly conduct; Disorderly conduct can elevate to assault on a government official; Assault on a government official can result in the inability to secure future jobs. The domino affect now impacts how you live, eat and provide for your family. Is it worth it? Never. Control your emotions. Manage your choices. Survive the Stop.

For several years I allowed one of my son's friends to live in my home because he had no other alternatives. I treated him as my son and shared with him the many lessons and guidance that I provide to the young men who are my blood lineage. Recently, I got a call from the young man thanking me for the sound wisdom I had provided to him over the years because it proved life-saving just moments before he called me. On a drive from one location to another, the young man was stopped by a law enforcement professional. He said to me, "Pops, I should have been arrested and riding in the back of the police car right now." He told me he was indeed wrong. Because he recently has been without work he was unable to secure proper tags and a driver's license. He was driving illegally. When the officer pulled him over he was very cooperative and followed the guidance I impart to you now. He humbled himself and was truthful with the officer. The officer in that very moment showed mercy on the young man, told him to take care of his license, outstanding tickets and get himself together. Because of the young man's respect and demeanor, the officer used his discretion on how to handle the situation. I am thankful that this young man survived the stop – in more ways than one. You have the same ability.

In my more than 30 years of work in law enforcement, I have heard tale after tale of officers determining what their next steps and actions are based on the behavior of the person they have stopped. Again, while you cannot control what the other person does you do have some impact and influence on how things in your encounter proceed. Remember the ultimate goal is to leave the encounter with your life and the least amount of damage possible.

When speaking with an informant about his activities for the last couple of years, he revealed to me that he was traveling from Atlanta to North Carolina and was stopped by an officer. In that moment he faced the realization that he might be going to jail. As his eyes began to constrict, the blood flowed faster and his heart began to race, he pondered the notion that he most definitely could not outrun the radio alerts that would broadcast his whereabouts. He could not outrun the police car that would most assuredly go after him in high speed pursuit. All of those things he realized would cost him much more than an arrest – more fines, more lawyer fees, more charges and quite possibly his life. He decided his one, last option was to remain calm and use his words.

He put his hands on the steering wheel where the officer could see them. When the officer asked for his license and registration he openly admitted that he knew he was speeding, he has points on his license for his previous offenses and his automobile insurance is extremely high. The officer asked him where he was going and why was he driving so fast. The informant stated that he was trying to get home and didn't realize he was speeding until he saw the blue lights flashing in the rear-view mirror. He told the officer he realized he was doing his job, thanked him for keeping the highways safe and asked him if there was any way he could show him mercy to avoid further fines and increased insurance he would greatly appreciate it. The officer did write him a ticket and told him to get home safely. Based on the informant's history, the outcome could have been totally different. It was his respectful demeanor that allowed him to Survive the Stop. Your focus, desire and demeanor should be the same.

The Ultmate Goal:

Leave the encounter with your life.

Secondary Goals:

- Leave the encounter without inflicting bodily harm or injury.

- Leave the encounter without receiving bodily harm or injury

- Manage your emotions and communication.

- Avoid being arrested.

- Reduce the likelihood of additional tickets, court costs and points on your insurance.

KNOW WHAT YOU NEED TO KNOW: UNDERSTANDING THE PROCESS

It is imperative that you understand what can take place within the traffic stop. This is essential because how you position yourself with the officer plays a vital role in the severity or leniency the officer has the authority to extend at his discretion. There are six key things that can happen during a traffic stop. Recognizing and embracing these can make a huge difference in your outcome. The six possible outcomes include a verbal conversation or verbal warning, a written warning, a ticket or citation, an arrest, a physical altercation or the loss of life. As much as possible, your aim is to remain within the first three possibilities.

Will it Remain JUST WORDS? Verbal Warning

The verbal conversation which may lead to a verbal warning is your best possible outcome. When pulled over in your automobile by a law enforcement professional, how you conduct yourself within the conversation directly impacts how quickly and how severely the reaction of the officer is likely to be. Within the conversation your goal is to be polite and respectful to elicit the same response from the officer. When you are honest and courteous the likelihood of you exiting the communication with only a verbal warning is increased exponentially. Examples of verbal warnings might include anything from take care of your tickets, get your license renewed, update your registration or slow down. A verbal warning carries no penalties or paper trail and it is your most desirable outcome. Remember, it often depends on you.

It's Only a Piece of Paper - Written Warning

The written warning is a document which contains the details of your infraction, however, like the verbal warning, it is not accompanied with penalties or a paper trail that has an adverse effect on your driving record, insurance or other elements of your capacity to drive or operate a motor vehicle. Officers also have the ability to determine how they will handle your specific situation and often are prompted on how to proceed by what you say and how you say it in your conversation with them. At the forefront of your mind should always be the end you get your most desired outcome. This means, you making a conscious choice to maintain self-discipline and emotional control. As you receive and give information proceed to achieve your goal – as few ramifications and repercussions as possible.

A colleague of mine with whom I worked in the bureau for 14 years tells of his time as a State Trooper in Miami, Florida. He stopped a local Disc Jockey early one morning traveling 90 miles per hour. As a State Trooper, he stopped the man and asked him why he was traveling at such a high rate of speed. He informed him that not only was he endangering his own life but he was also putting others in jeopardy. The DJ admitted that he was having some personal issues. He informed the state trooper that he was late to work at the radio station and that they were playing loops (pre-recorded music and promos) until he arrived. Because of the honesty and sincerity of the man he had stopped, the State Trooper made the decision to let the man go with a written warning. He informed the DJ that this was not an everyday occurrence. He instructed him to slow down, be careful and be mindful of his own safety and the safety of those around him. The DJ thanked the state trooper profusely and was on his way to the radio station. If the DJ had been rude or disrespectful to the officer, the outcome would have been markedly different. Your outcomes, too, are impacted by your attitude and demeanor.

It Just Got Expensive - Ticket or Citation

A ticket or citation is issued during a traffic stop when there is some type of violation. This could be a moving violation or it could be in direct relation to some other law that has been broken. Please know, even as I am sharing with you the most effective ways to ensure you Survive the Stop and come out with the least amount of damage, there will more times than not be officers who issue a written ticket or citation. It is what they are hired to do. It is what they are sworn to do. Additionally, you may encounter an officer who does not respond to your impolite words or disrespectful comments. But as you drove away, he made a note on the back of the ticket that the District Attorney will most assuredly see and possibly determine how they will proceed with you in the court room. It can be the difference in you receiving a Prayer for Judgement or the full maximum penalty for your infraction.

Your attitude can cost you. The notable point for you is even if your stop does result in a written ticket or citation, practice respect and humility so that this is the last of the six stages you encounter in your traffic stop. At all costs – Survive the Stop.

Your Life Just Changed Completely - Physical Altercation

Many years ago when I was a police officer in the city where I was born and raised, I stopped a guy on Interstate 40 for speeding. This was during a time period when "wine coolers" were extremely popular. As I approached the car carefully and looked into the driver's seat I noticed he had a wine cooler between his legs. In addition to speeding, he now had to contend with the fact that having open alcohol in a moving vehicle is against the law. As I came close enough to the man for me to speak to him and for him to hear me, he immediately began to be aggressive in his verbal communication and in his mannerisms. He disrespectfully told me to hurry up and do what I have to do because he has a family member in the hospital sick. I could smell the alcohol on his breath and was increasingly more concerned of his inability to drive safely. I instructed him to get out of the car for a sobriety test. He became extremely combative to the point of physical aggression.

This traffic stop for speeding was now attached to open alcohol and escalated swiftly to an all-out brawl on the side of the road. Listen, if an officer has stopped you for a legal reason – whether their reason for stopping you is true or false, if they have stopped you – the time to debate it is not on the side of the road. A physical altercation is not what you want. A physical altercation can lead to you being tazed, an experience I do not wish upon anyone. A physical altercation can cause you to be doused with pepper spray. This too is a method officers are authorized to use which inhibits your ability to see, breathe and function normally. A physical altercation can lead to literal fist fight which can lead you badly injured at the hands of another person. And likely the most damaging of a physical altercation is you end up being shot.

Remember, the side of the road is not the place for you to initiate a disrespectful discussion or physical alteration – the officer is going to be "right." Please know that right does not always mean who is or is not dispensing truth. Right in this situation has to do with who has the authority whether it is physical authority or jurisdictional authority. Your focus – Survive the Stop. Debate the merits of the stop through your attorney or in front of a judge.

The Personal Escort You Want to Avoid - Arrest

When conducting a traffic stop, there are times when the stop will accelerate to an arrest. Contrary to popular belief, when an officer signs on to his tour of duty with a 1041 code to the dispatch center, his main goal at the end of his tour is to report 1042 to the dispatch. (Code 1041 is the tour has started. Code 1042 is end of tour, going home.) Officers do not want to spend any portion of the tour at the hospital. Neither do they want to have to make a visit to the jail. Not hospital, not jail, not anything that has to do with a mountain of paperwork or a ton of professional or public scrutiny. While arrests are a part of the officer's job and it may unfortunately be something you one day have to experience, remain calm, be respectful, refrain from any additional charges being added to the reason for your arrest and stop and ensure that you Survive the Stop.

Things Will Never Be the Same - Loss of Life

One of the greatest tragedies an officer can experience is a physical altercation escalating to a loss of life. One of the saddest experiences for a citizen is the loss of a loved one because of +the events of a traffic stop. If you have ever been involved in a traffic stop on either side of the blue lights, loss of life is one of the last things you believe you will have a conversation about or want to have a conversation about when the interaction is over. Loss of life never means the interaction is over, it is the start of a continual conversation and existence of pain and damage. Yet, it can happen so quickly if you are not aware of the six potential actions that can happen inside of a traffic stop.

So many times we are inundated a traffic stop turned deadly. Throughout my career, I would review the footage of traffic stops for training and development. I remember the footage of a State Trooper who conducted a traffic stop. This Trooper pulled over a car which contained two men of Hispanic descent. The Trooper followed the prescribed procedures for a traffic stop, collected information through a conversation with the two men and continued the process by returning to his official vehicle. The two men became very anxious as they were illegal immigrants. Their fear of being deported back to Mexico became so overwhelming to them that they decided to act in an unlawful manner to ensure their presence in the United States would not be interrupted by this Special Agent.

As the Trooper completed his required tasks in his car, he got out of the automobile and headed back to the car where the two men were. They jumped out of the car and charged toward him with the intent of attacking him, overtaking him and fleeing. One thing to note, an officer in any division of law enforcement wants to get safely home every night just like you. I assure you he would rather be tried by 12 than carried by six. Defending his life when under attack is human nature and a part of his training. As the two men charged at him full force the Trooper pulled his weapon and shot both of the individuals. One of the men did survive. The other resulted in a loss of life. Whatever the situation, it is never worth your life.

BEFORE THE STOP: PREPARE FOR THE LEAST AMOUNT OF MONETARY AND PHYSICAL DAMAGE

Once those blue lights start flashing, there are a number of things that lend to a peaceful and productive stop. Even before then, you want to be mindful of a few key elements. First, your body will have a physiological response. Your heart will begin to beat a bit faster, your hands may start to sweat and you may feel nervousness or anxiety in your body. Fear or concern for the unknown is an underlying factor here; it is normal.

Often as the driver, you will become agitated because you have somewhere to be or you do not want to deal with the hassle that you perceive goes along with being involved in a traffic stop. Depending on the time of day, the spider senses of the officer are operating at a much higher and more intense rate. The officer is having to contend with the fact that it may be night, the location is not well lit and it is on the side of the road. They are also considering whether it is a country road, is back up-coming quickly if they need to and will it take a considerable amount of time for assistance to arrive. The officer also has to weigh the balance of more than one person occupying the car. When multiple people are present in the vehicle they may have to approach with even more caution and may experience apprehension until they feel safe. More experienced officers may feel more of a sense of readiness.

Before the stop, stay aware of the fact that all of your movements should be subtle. Everything you do should be done with the least amount of movement. Know that the officer is a living, breathing being with reactions - just like you. The officer's comfort depends on their years of experience, the number of traffic stops they have conducted and their level of confidence in this situation and in their job in its entirety.

SPECIAL NOTE: Law enforcement professionals are human beings tasked with performing a superhuman job. They are expected to perform a job to perfection in an imperfect world with imperfect people.

The law enforcement professional has to do things most human beings don't want to do. Most people are at home in bed. The officer is out in the dead of the might in the middle of nowhere.

Law enforcement professional have one of the most vital jobs; they separate order from anarchy. Without them there would be total anarchy and chaos. Law enforcement is the line that keeps the appearance of balance in our society.

When everyone else is running away from mayhem and disorder – law enforcement professionals must run toward it. They have the great task of serving and protecting regardless of the circumstances – rain, sleet, snow, danger, threats, bodily harm, injury, death. Before the traffic stop – keep these things in mind and act accordingly.

As the officer approaches your vehicle, they don't know you teach Sunday School and they don't know you are a model citizen. All they have to go on is the information that is provided from the system and their interaction with you. Contrary to popular belief, no traffic stop is routine. This is true because no two people are the same and no two situations are the same. The moment the officer assumes all traffic stops are routine it is the moment he loses his edge and possibly his life. As the driver, you should also keep in mind that he must approach every situation with a new outlook and a fresh set of eyes. Doing the due diligence of the stop is imperative. Respect that.

As the driver, prepare yourself mentally. Breathe. Begin to speak to yourself in a manner that is positive and keeps you focused on your desired outcomes. You will say things like: I am going to survive. I am going to get through this. I am going to remain calm. I will Survive the Stop. Essential actions that merit repeating that you should be focused on before the stop:

- Be polite.

- Be mannerable.

- Be accommodating.

- Change the atmosphere.

What exactly do I mean when I say change the atmosphere? This is not a confrontation, but a meeting. In a meeting you present yourself in a positive way. During this meeting, yield to the officer. Remember we have an ultimate goal that we want you to achieve – Survive the Stop with the least amount of damages. Your aim is to cause the officer to see you as non-threatening as possible. The officer seeing you as non-threating is important because you must always keep in mind that this is a human being with emotions. They are highly trained professionals but they are still human beings.

As you are waiting for the officer to approach the car, the reason it is taking him time to get to the car is because he is checking the license plate, matching the tag to the car, making sure the registration is current and getting prepared to approach. This is the perfect time for you to gather your thoughts and prepare your positive personality to respect his authority and jurisdiction. It is all about Surviving the Stop.

THE ACTUAL STOP: JUST STOP – STOP THE CAR, STOP TALKING, STOP NEGATIVE COMMENTS AND BEHAVIOR

You glance into the rearview mirror and you see the blue lights flashing. A few moments later you hear the sound of the siren. As you pull to the side of the road you brace yourself as the actual stop is about to occur.

During this time the officer is gathering their thoughts. This is also the time for you to get yourself ready for the encounter. Breathe deeply and calm yourself. Your aim at this moment is to remain relaxed and realize that you might be about to hear some questions you may or may not want to answer.

Officer Gathering Data on You and the Automobile

At this point the officer is gathering data from the system. This includes data on the vehicle as well as the person who might be associated with the vehicle. The vehicle license tag is an important tool at this juncture because the license tag lets the officer know who is the holder of the insurance, who the vehicle is registered to and what vehicle the license tag should be on. If all of these elements do not match, you will be asked a series of questions. After these questions are asked and answered, the officer will go back to their vehicle and investigate. The officer is working to determine is the vehicle stolen, is the tag correct or being used improperly, who should the automobile be registered to.

As it relates to you as the driver, the officer puts the license and registration into the system to garner information on you. The system is cross checking your name for warrants. The officer will also have access to information concerning who you are, where you live while matching the system to the information he has about you in hand. If everything matches with the system you may get a warning or a citation. If the items do not match further questions and investigations will occur.

Officer Checking Surroundings

As the actual stop commences the officer is also checking the surroundings. There are many key elements that go into how and where the officer will pull you over. The stop requires him to inform Dispatch where he is and what is about to take place. They will let the command center know exactly where they are. The alert that they are on Interstate 40 at mile marker 72 is extremely important. I40 stretches at minimum from North Carolina to California. The command center must know where the officer is for your safety and for theirs.

The officer is also observing the car to determine the number of occupants inside the automobile. The number of occupants also helps the determination of a safe place to stop for you and him. As the officer ushers you to the side of road they will let you know where to park so the stop can be conducted safely. The officer is also taking into account who is with you, where you are, who is around.

When the lights flash – pull over. You do not need to determine where the safe place is. The officer has already taken that into consideration. If the law enforcement professional deems it necessary for you to move after you have pulled over he will give instructions over the intercom to pull down further, pull in a parking lot, pull out of traffic or whatever is safest. Let the officer instruct you on what to do. Whatever you do – do not, I repeat – do not drive another six or seven blocks. When this occurs the officer may deduce that you are hiding something and you are taking extra time to conceal something illegal. The officer may also believe that you are fleeing. Then other officers become involved. You have most likely also been successful at – well – pissing him off and you have now started your communication exchange digging yourself out of a hole. It is not worth it. Pull over.

As the Officer Approaches

As the officer approaches they are watching the inside of the car. In the words of mothers and grandmothers with great wisdom – be still and be quiet. The officer is paying close attention to you and the other passengers. This is not the time to be moving around. Save your dance moves for the family reunion or the class reunion. Refrain from searching for documents and making sudden movements. All the officer sees, especially at night, is shadows. If you are moving around the law enforcement professional is working extra hard to determine what you and the other passengers are doing, if you have weapons and whether or not you are hiding something.

His decision on which side of the car he approaches may be related to traffic or other environmental elements. Either way – be still and be quiet.

When the Officer Arrives at Your Door

When the officer arrives at your door, resist the urge to speak. Refrain from speaking as you listen, follow instructions, answer questions.

Keep hands visible. Place your hands on the steering wheel as soon as you pull the car over and place it in park.

Look the officer in the eye. This is not a staring contest. Look the officer in the eye respectfully.

Address the officer by title. Look at their badge and say the name – Officer Smith, Trooper Smith.

Allow the Officer to do Their Job

Again, every officer's job is to protect and serve. In this case the job at hand is to enforce motor vehicle laws. Think about when you are authorized to do a job. There are days when you are able to do it effectively and efficiently because those you serve or work with allow you to do what you have been chosen and trained to do. Then there are days when it is much more difficult because you are receiving push back and resistance from supervisors, co-workers or those you serve. You simply want to do the job you are authorized to do with respect. The same is with the officer. During the actual stop – allow the office to do the job.

The actual stop is not as harsh and dangerous as the results have shown to be. What makes the stop dangerous is in large part related to your response to the officer. Your actions will determine what the next steps will become. It is indeed an interaction; your interaction will determine the outcome. If you put negativity into the interaction – it is what you will receive.

Failure to stop, often referred to as a rolling stop is a common reason people are pulled over. This simple stop by a police officer can be a quick and easy exit. A response like "you ain't got nothing else to do" can escalate to disorderly conduct. A polite and honest response like, "sir, I thought I did stop completely," can result in a warning at least or at most a ticket for that infraction. Respond in a positive light and you get the same in return. Allow the officer to do his job.

Officers are people with emotions and they will often give back to you what you give to them. At the stop you have more to lose than they do – they are holding the chips. Understand the actual stop and Survive the Stop.

THE MEETING OF PERSONALITIES: TWO WORLDS CAN COLLABORATE OR COLLIDE

As you prepare to meet someone that you've probably never met in the capacity you're about to meet them remain aware that the officer in the uniform is occupied by a human being. Some emotions and sensory preceptors are beginning to intensify for you and for the officer. Keep your mind open to the concept that the procedures of the department are the same but the officers are different and the personalities are different.

There are some officers who will be stone faced. They will be strictly business when they come into contact with you. There are some officers who will exchange pleasantries. They will bid you good morning and ask how you are before they follow the procedures. Your assignment is to interact in a way that is beneficial to you. The officer will observe your personality and how you present yourself. Presenting yourself in a manner that is rude by demanding that they go on and write the ticket because you have to go or offering a kind good afternoon typically is the mitigating factor in how you are handled.

Everything you do in life is directly related to your personality and your personality directly affects every relationship you have long term and short term. Your personality affects how you approach every relationship including this one. Because you have so much riding on this relationship, you must make sure your personality is amicable, easygoing and accommodating.

Have you ever been in a place of business and encountered someone who was rude and did not speak? Have you ever had the daunting task of working with a know-it-all? Have you ever been on the receiving end of someone telling you how to do your job and they have little if any knowledge or experience with who you are, what you do and what your goals and objectives are? What is your perception of this person and how do you deal with them moving forward? These are the same questions for you to ponder when you come into contact with an officer during a traffic stop.

How you perceive other people is extremely important; It governs how you treat them. Along the same lines, how you are perceived by an officer is extremely important. You have met people who are rude and disrespectful. Once you get to know them you come to accept that that's just how they are. An officer doesn't have the time investment to decipher that personality and make exceptions long term. You need to give the personality impression that you want used to determine the end result of this communication exchange.

If you have ever heard yourself say, "this is just how I am," then you know your flaws. If you have a smart mouth – you know it. Go inside yourself. Are you constantly told you are arrogant? Do you get reminded you can be an SOB sometimes? Are you first cousins with the donkey? You know your own personality better than anyone. In this meeting of personalities, become the opposite. It really is this simple:

- Be mannerable and respectful.

- Practice saying yes sir and yes ma'am.

- Smile.

- Be pleasant.

- Exude positivity.

  And if you can't do any of those things:

- KEEP YOUR MOUTH SHUT.

- Be polite:

  - Yes.

  - No.

  - Follow commands.

  - KEEP YOUR MOUTH SHUT.

It seems we shouldn't have to review and say these things specifically – but apparently we do.

Remember: you want something. What is the end goal? What you want and what you get is largely determined by what happens when your personality meets theirs.

You want to leave unscathed – how do you do that. Being rude? Using profanity? Telling the officer how to do their job? No.

Once you ask yourself the question about what your end goal is and you have the answer – proceed in that direction.

If you've been given a license to drive in any of the 50 United States – you have a certain ability to maneuver physical and intellectually. Then you also have the ability to develop the skillset to maneuver within whatever personality you come into contact with as it relates to law enforcement. If you choose not to develop or apply that skillset, you can be certain that your personality and that of the officer will clash. Once that takes place the results are irreversible. At least be honest with yourself about your intentions to Survive the Stop. But if you truly want to make a conscious decision about the impact a traffic stop can have on your personal, professional and financial life make the meeting of personalities as pleasant as possible.

Believe me, the vast majority of officers don't wake up in the morning looking for people to harass. It is not in the core of their personality. They don't start their tour with the intent to physically assault or shoot someone. There are too many ramifications – personal and professional. There is too much paperwork and too much backlash. The officer is looking for a specific result just like you. BUT – he has a job to do. Don't make him do his job. His job entails a verbal command. The verbal command can lead to non-lethal force. Non-lethal force can lead to lethal force. As the officer goes up each step on the stair case – the job responsibilities increase. Now, we have a real problem.

The nature of your outcome or problem in large part depends upon you. Results are what you get when you follow the rules. Consequences are the results of negative choices. Your thoughts become your actions. Your thoughts should be focused on what you desire.

In the meeting of personalities and in the midst of difficult situations please keep in mind the notion of might and right. When might and right unite you can rarely win. In the story of David and Goliath, David the little shepherd boy was right while Goliath the terrible giant had might. There is no way in the world that the little shepherd boy should have been able to defeat the giant with a rock and a sling shot, but he had the power of righteous so he prevailed. In the meeting of personalities the officer represents might. He has the power of the police department, the city and department resources as well as the government on his side. If you couple that with the fact that you may have committed some type of violation the likelihood of you coming out unscathed is probably unfavorable.

Now, if you believe that you have not committed a violation and you do want to defend yourself, the place to do that is in a court room and not on the shoulder of the road. Even in this case, when the personalities meet – you want to be positive while being right. Aggression begets aggression. Do people respond to aggression positively or negatively? Typically negatively. Think positive to get the results desired or at minimum the least amount of damages. Survive the Stop.

YOU CONTROL YOU: YOUR ATTITUDE, MANNERISMS AND TONE

Your attitude, mannerisms and tone shape the interaction between you and the officer when you have been pulled over during a traffic stop. A portion of how you act and react is born out of a defense mechanism which is prompted by your previous interactions with officers or by the image that has been portrayed to you by family, media, community and any other individual or collection of individuals who has direct or indirect influence over you. Refrain from being defensive on the side of the road. For many of us, attitude, mannerisms and tone is simply a way of life for ux. This is how we communicate and respond with everyone.

You have been living your life long enough to know what your specific character flaws are. You have been told numerous times by your family, friends, co-workers and employers areas where you need improvement. If you know that you are aggressive – withhold your aggressive communication on the side of the road. If you know you have a sharp tongue – taper it when you have an exchange with an officer. If you have been told repeatedly that your words and delivery are interpreted as rude and disrespectful, tame your tongue during a traffic stop. How you present yourself both verbally and non-verbally plays a huge part in how the officer proceeds during the traffic stop. Know that you have the power to alter the situation for the better or for worse; make a conscious choice to practice self-control with your communication.

Mr./Ms. Aggressive

A number of years ago during one of the most volatile times in our country's history, I sat on a panel to have a public discussion about the state of affairs between law enforcement and the community. I was completely shocked and disgusted that one of the people on the panel not only instructed a room filled with angry, emotional, impressionable people to be aggressive any time they are stopped by law enforcement. I was even more astonished at the hundreds of people who sat attentively to his accounts of HOW to aggressively behave toward law enforcement during communication exchanges. Aggressive behavior and aggressive communication will cause you consequences that you do not want to contend with on the side of the road or in the court room.

Aggressive Comments and Responses:

- "Write the ticket – I have somewhere to be."

- "You don't have to explain all that to me. Just do what you got to do."

- "I bet if you didn't have that gun you wouldn't be so tough."

- "Let me catch you somewhere without that badge and see just how tough you are then Mr. Officer."

Mr./Ms. Sarcastic

If you are the person known for your quick wit and smart comments – save it. During a traffic stop is not the time for you to be sarcastic. It takes on a tone of disrespect whether you intend for it to or not. Sarcasm is a conscious or unconscious attempt to minimize another person's authority. This type of approach is not a help to you. It is a hindrance. You are best served to use your communication skills answering questions, being direct but polite and refraining from unsolicited comments and off-color remarks.

Sarcastic Comments and Responses:

- "Shouldn't you be out be arresting someone really doing something wrong?"

- "While you're here bothering me you just missed the Hot Now sign come on at Krispy Kreme."

- "Dunkin Doughnuts has a special going on right now. I have a coupon I can give you if you hurry up and stop wasting my time and yours.

Please know, comedy clubs have open mic nights where you can go and practice your comedic skills instead of with an officer performing his job. Sarcasm during a traffic stop will be rewarded back in the form of a ticket or citation. Withhold your sarcastic comments and demeanor.

Mr./Ms. Know it All

You may have a great depth and breadth of knowledge and experience in your profession and in many other areas. The time to assert this knowledge is not during a traffic stop. One of the biggest questions I recommend you asking yourself is how can you know something you have never done or experienced. If we take a moment and be very candid and honest, if you knew so much you wouldn't have been speeding or would not have got caught. Making it a point to wield your perceived knowledge during a traffic stop with an individual who is trained, experienced and practices the tenants of the profession every day is most assuredly not the proper time or approach.

Imagine that you go to work every day and you have mastered your job or at minimum you have developed your own best practices to operate effectively and efficiently based on the guidelines you have been given and the expectations that have been placed before you. Now imagine that you have a co-worker or random visitor who has only observed you do your job in passing or read a few books and articles on your profession. Yet, they feel compelled to tell you how to do your job and scrutinize you every step of the way. If the vast majority of your knowledge comes from television programs and internet videos, your knowledge base is no match for the officer who is skilled and trained. Truthfully, it doesn't need to be. There is no need to match intellect or brain power. Simply answer the questions, follow the instructions and Survive the Stop.

"Know-It-All" Comments and Responses:

- "I know what the law says – I don't need you to tell me."

- "I can go 10 mph over the speed limit and not get a speeding ticket."

- "I know what you can and can't ask me. I don't have to tell you nothing."

- "I know what you can and cannot do concerning my rights."

Mr./Ms. Work the System

The person who believes they have a penchant for working the system can actually end up in a worse situation by trying to manipulate the officer or the circumstances. One of the most common ways people attempt to work the system is by name dropping. They aim to use the connections they have with other people to alter the outcome of the traffic stop in their favor. People will directly or indirectly mention the name of a person they perceive to be influential to intimidate the officer to react in a specific manner. Individuals will also use the names of others to impress the officer in order to gain a favorable outcome result. While it has been helpful for some people it ultimately is the wrong thing to do. While you may have a high opinion of an individual or group or you may have a perceived concept of the person's power or influence, this may have the opposite effect on the officer who is conducting the traffic stop.

Another popular tactic that fails more often than it works is the Beauty and the Beast technique. This is when an individual will use flirting, showing skin, exposing body parts, initiating covert illicit conversations to gain the upper hand and reduce or eliminate the possible consequences. It may be perceived to many that this is a viable approach, but it lessens your integrity and taints how the officer sees you. Always operate with the thought in mind that how you behave is a direct reflection of how the law enforcement professional will treat you. If you want to be treated with respect you must start the communication exchange with respect for yourself.

"Work the System" Actions and Behaviors:

- Flirting.

- Showing Skin.

- Exposing body parts inappropriately.

- Initiating illicit conversations.

Mr./Ms. Rude and Disrespectful

The driver who is rude and disrespectful to the sworn officer who has pulled them over is most likely to encounter a professional who is much more stern and much less lenient. The rude and disrespectful person must embrace the universal law of reaping and sowing. If you desire to be treated politely and professionally, your engagement with the officer must illustrate the same mannerisms during the entire encounter. The officer may not match you word for word and remark for remark, however, their next steps are often directly dependent upon your treatment of them. Not only are you creating an experience for yourself, you are also creating an experience for the officer. Their aim is always to conduct the business at hand as swiftly as possible. Your level of rudeness and disrespect creates an experience that will have lasting ramifications upon you long after the blue lights are off and they have traveled on down the highway. If you cannot respect the person in the uniform in front of you, at least respect your own present and future experience. Be polite and respectful.

Rude and Disrespectful Behavior:

- Telling the officer what he can and cannot do.

- Shoving your license into the officer's hands.

- Throwing registration information at the officer.

- Flinging documents out of the car window at the officer.

Mr./Ms. Combative

The combative person must realize that when they posture themselves in this manner they are waging exactly what the word denotes – combat. The side of the road is not the place to engross oneself or an officer in verbal or physical combat. Choosing words and the delivery of those words in a manner that creates a negative environment and undesirable outcome will have the greatest damaging impact on you – the driver. If you believe an injustice is being done to you, consult with an attorney and report the situation after you have safely left the traffic stop. Intentionally being combative will only get you enthralled in a battle you may not be equipped to win in that time and space reality. If you are unable to control your responses without being combative, answer the officer's questions completely and concisely so that your words are not mistaken for ammunition.

Combative Behavior:

- Everything the officer says, you have an answer that is the opposite of his directives.

- Giving word for word responses to everything the officer says.

- Cutting the officer off while he is speaking.

- Commanding the officer to take specific actions.

- Telling the officer what you will and will not do.

- Threatening to call the Police Chief.

Mr./Ms. Victim

Playing the victim, damsel in distress, woe is me characters may be the most ineffective and irritating approach to use on an officer. These are especially ineffective when the person being pulled over obviously has knowledge of their possible infraction. Positioning oneself in the "why me?" posture can cause the opposite outcome that you desire. The person who plays the victim will often proclaim that they did not do anything wrong. They will also displace the responsibility and to make it appear as though the officer is taking advantage of them. This type of stance only increases your ability to get additional infractions and decreases the likelihood that the officer will extend the mercy that he is allowed to at his discretion. You never have to play the victim. Take the responsibility for your choices, be honest and move forward in the traffic stop in a manner that will yield you the best possible outcomes.

The Victim Comments and Responses:

- "…because of what I am driving…"

- "…if I was on the other side of town…"

- "…if I was white…"

- "I was targeted."

- "You profiled me."

Mr./Ms. Deceptive

Okay, can we just be honest about lying. Some of you are pulled over in a traffic stop and before the officer even gets to your car door you have concocted a story that would sell millions at the box office. Then some of you wait until the officer gets within ear shot and you start fabricating a tale so poorly thought out that Dr. Seuss wouldn't allow it anywhere near Green Eggs and Ham in the library. Simply put – you're lying and you know you're lying. Period. Simply put – Just Stop It. One thing is for certain, if your false statements have any connection to the system set up to track motor vehicles and drivers, it is only a matter of time before you are found out in that very traffic stop. Why increase your ability to come out ahead and decrease your capacity to have influence on the officer when you know the lies you are telling are going to meet you face to face. Tell the truth. Be honest.

Deceptive Comments and Behaviors:

- "My license expired – they didn't send me the stuff to renew."

- "I moved and they haven't found me."

- "My wife was supposed to renew the tag – I thought she had already done it."

- "I mailed the insurance payment in more than a month ago and they said they still haven't got it."

- Car filled with marijuana smoke, you spray air freshener and argue with the police officer it is a cigar or a Black and Mild he smells and not marijuana.

- Everybody's fault but your own.

- Placing blame. Being deceptive. (You know what you do and say.)

Mr./Ms. Briber

There are those who will use their name, reputation, position, assets, worth, position in life and connections to get out of a sticky situation. If it is a card they believe they can play and win, they will throw it from the deck without hesitation. If you do this in any form, it is considered bribery. Offering or suggesting material items of favors in exchange for leniency puts you and the officer in a precarious position. Remember, the officer has the authority to practice leniency without your open or hidden suggestions of what you can and will do for them. Flashing a light on shiny objects is not the route you want to take. Instead, use the same charm and respect to answer the questions, explain the situation and ask for compassion in whatever your situation is. In these instances where a bribe is offered you taint your own integrity and put the integrity of the officer in jeopardy. Neither is worth it.

Briber Comments and Responses:

- "Hey. I'm the owner of XYZ restaurant. Didn't I see you there a few times this past month? Come on by and I'll make sure you and your guests are taken care of whenever you come."

- "You look like a golf man. You know I'm part owner at the new course they just built. Come on by and let me get you hooked up with a free membership."

- "Good to see you. You know I had lunch with the police chief last week. Some great work you all are doing in the community with your new initiatives."

THE OFFICER'S AUTHORITY: LET THEM DO THEIR JOB, YOU DO YOUR PART

As a sworn officer, the individual wearing the badge is certified and authorized to carry out the enforcement of laws for the city, municipality, state, college campus or other qualifying entity. The sworn officer has the legal authority to enforce traffic laws, civil laws and ordinances. The mission of all law enforcement officers is to protect and serve citizens within the community.

As we take a look at the authority of an officer, let's first consider the delicate job that they have chosen to perform. First and foremost there are no do-overs. Every decision that an officer makes will affect them directly or indirectly. In your job responsibilities and most other professions, you and others typically have the opportunity to take a couple of days to think and make decisions. Officers must process and make decisions instantly. An officer's authority is tried and tested constantly. An officer's conduct must consistently be beyond reproach.

Let's just say, you drive through the light playing with your phone. You cross over into the other lane and other drivers are swerving to keep from getting hit by you. You drive up on the curve and have people jumping off bicycles to save their own lives from you poor choices. The officer wants to say and probably should say what in the world is wrong with you – in much more abrasive and much less filtered terms. You need it and deserve it. However, the officer can't. An officer reprimanding you in that manner can cause him a write-up, disciplinary action and possibly the loss of his job. You have clearly violated several laws and put you and other people in harm's way but because his actions are undoubtedly held to a different standard than most his authority is also under scrutiny.

Think about the last time you watched a newscast and all of the violence and criminal acts that are reported on a daily basis. Rarely do you hear the reporter say CPA charged with assault on a client. Seldom do you hear the court reporter say hair stylist found guilty of communicating a threat. You will always here the radio, television, social media and other reports clearly specify the alleged or actual wrong doing of an officer. The actions of sworn officers are always placed under a more powerful microscope. As well they should be – to whom much is given, much is required. But if indeed all are going to expect and require more from officers, their authority should have the same level of respect and credence.

In my own work as a police officer I have stopped men who were shaving while operating a two ton motor vehicle. I have pulled over women putting on make-up traveling 50 mph. And while so many believe that because they have been driving for so long and know there automobiles so well, these are actions for which people can and should be pulled over yet they fail to respect the officer's authority as he is working to protect and serve.

Part of the officer's authority is created to keep you safe and other people safe. The officer has the legal right to do the job. When you are pulled over please know that his job is to enforce the law. You do have a choice about what you will and will not do concerning the law. But if you find yourself in a situation where the officer is mandated to pull you over in a traffic stop he is legally within his authority to say, "Ma'am, license and registration." Survive the Stop. Comply with the authority.

One final thing that I must make crystal clear that is blatantly overlooked and ignored. Law enforcement officers position themselves as the line that separates chaos from order. When chaos appears in your home, on your job, in your community, in your church, at your educational institutions, in your own head – the law enforcement officer is the one who is dispatched. When slight inconveniences or total disruptions emerge in your personal or professional lives you want the authority of a law enforcement officer. Ask yourself, how can you love order and peace but you despise the people who are authorized to keep the peace? You love them as long as the order being kept is not toward you. Respect the authority in whatever form or venue it comes. It is designed to protect you and others. Allow it.

AFTERWORDS:
FATHERS AND LEADERS SPEAK

For years, fathers like me have needed a book like this, a book that talks about how to exercise control while you feel out of control.

"Surviving the Stop," the title says it all. At last, a thoughtful, straightforward dialogue aimed at helping motorists survive the encounter with law enforcement professionals.

It has become an all too common occurrence in the news where events around being stopped by law enforcement professionals escalate out of control. The person ends up dead or seriously injured. The law enforcement professional's reputation, along with those of the law enforcement community, is often tarnished beyond repair.

I am an African American father with three sons. Since their teenage years and on into adulthood, they have been stopped by law enforcement professionals over 100 times. It has been my fear that one day, an encounter with law enforcement during a traffic stop would escalate out of control. It has been my responsibility to teach them how their behavior and language can have a positive or negative effect on an already tense situation. I have tried to help them understand how their behavior is a catalyst that shapes someone else's experience. This is especially important when the other person is a law enforcement professional. My sons and my family have been fortunate. No encounters with law enforcement professionals have resulted in any serious outcomes. Now my sons have sons of their own. Now, they are trying to teach their sons what they learned from me. They, like me, are learning to hold their breath as their sons come of age where they interact with society and with law enforcement in particular.

For years, fathers like me have needed a book like this, a book that talks about how to exercise control while you feel out of control. We each have a personal responsibility to understand that our behavior is constantly creating an influence on those around us. Our actions do not occur in a vacuum. We must consider how the behavior of others may be influenced by how we respond when we see those blue lights in our rearview mirror. What behaviors do we need to exhibit so as not further intensify the encounter? What moves are suspicious? What language is disrespectful or inflammatory? What behaviors will cause the tension to build? What can we do to reduce that tension and deescalate the situation?

I am truly grateful for Retired Senior Special agent Bobby Kimbrough for helping fathers like me, my sons, and every motorist learn how to survive the stop.

Robert Johnson
Robert D. Johnson, President of JohnsonGROUP Consulting
Member of the Duke University Corporate Education Network
CEO Space International Faculty

What should I say? What should I do? What shouldn't I say? What shouldn't I do? ... stories, facts, and practical advice ... to educate us outside of law enforcement about how to minimize or prevent the loss of property or our life...

I often hear people—from teens and young adults to parents and grandparents--share that one of their most difficult decisions these days is what to read and what to throw away. In my opinion, <u>Surviving the Stop</u> is a must read for every person who potentially may be stopped by a law enforcement officer for a traffic violation or more serious complaint, or the parent or grandparent of someone who may be so stopped. What should I say? What should I do? What shouldn't I say? What shouldn't I do? Bobby Kimbrough provides stories, facts, and practical advice through the eyes and experience of a 25-year veteran of law enforcement to educate us outside of law enforcement about how to minimize or prevent the loss of property or our life if we are stopped by an officer of the law.

I am one of many, many people who have the privilege of calling Bobby Kimbrough a friend and all of us enjoy spending time with this extraordinary man. I also had the opportunity earlier in my life to room with a police officer for one year and learned first-hand that we law abiding citizens are insulated from a segment of our society few of us outside of law enforcement ever encounter face-to-face: the criminal element. If we truly understood the pressure, stress, and actual danger these men and women in uniform face on a daily basis, most of us would appreciate them more. So if and when we find ourselves stopped for a traffic violation, this book guides us in how to survive the stop in a unique, logical, and compelling way.

Harry P. Lay, President
Lay Professional Services, Inc.

THE FINAL WORD
BOBBY F. KIMBROUGH, JR.

You have the power and the ability to Survive the Stop.

In every area of your life...

Change the Atmosphere, Change the Outcome.

ABOUT THE AUTHORS

Bobby F. Kimbrough, Jr.

A law enforcement and security professional for more than 30 years, Bobby F. Kimbrough, Jr. is a dedicated professional committed to serving his country and his community. His work with local, national and international agencies has afforded him the opportunity to directly and indirectly impact the lives of millions.

As a Special Agent for the US Department of Justice for more than 20 years, Kimbrough specialized in crimes against the government which includes organized crime, money laundering, drug trafficking and gangs. He was a certified Department of Justice Instructor with other certifications and trainings reserved for the US government's most elite personnel. His professional endeavors afforded him the opportunity to travel extensively to all 50 of the United States of America. A fluent speaker of the Spanish language, Kimbrough's diverse background has opened doors for work internationally; He was a member of the Foreign Operations Group which functioned throughout the Caribbean. Kimbrough is known throughout the region by local, state and federal law enforcement for his interview skills, techniques and results. Kimbrough received a degree in Sociology from High Point University.

As a community leader and businessman, Kimbrough provides specialized training in security concepts and safety measures for various industries. The founder and Chief Executive Officer of Unified Security Solutions, Kimbrough's management team has more than 65 years of combined experience. The firm is committed to providing security solutions which span from a physical presence at a designated location, indoor and outdoor physical evaluation to include recommendations and solutions for preventative measures as well as training for staff and volunteers. As a committed father and avid volunteer with young people, Kimbrough knows the importance and has seen firsthand the harvest of planting seeds in the minds of young people. Because of this, in November 2013 he founded Branded For Knowledge. BFK, Inc. is an exclusive, high-end clothing apparel company, which spreads positive messages of influence for current and future generations to understand and embrace the importance of knowledge and education.

Because of his expansive reach and influence, he is a devoted philanthropist giving money to and raising money for numerous charities, non-profit organizations, churches and scholarship funds. A highly sought-after speaker, his insight blazes the path to enlightenment in the areas of leadership, success and achievement as well as overcoming personal and professional obstacles.

With a deeply rooted desire to offer alternatives to young men who Kimbrough often encounters in his work, he created MAPS – Men Against the Prison System. This program has met such phenomenal response that it was duplicated and expanded to include high schools and middle schools in various school systems. Because of his burning desire to eliminate the number of boys and young men who become involved with the criminal justice system and encourage others to find the greatness within themselves, Kimbrough serves as a motivationalist speaking to organizations, churches and reentry groups.

Bobby F. Kimbrough was husband to the late Clementine Kimbrough for 15 years. Among his accomplishments, he considers being a single parent raising seven boys to be responsible, respectful, reverent young men his absolute greatest. Without question, his legacy shall be continually perpetuated through his biological and professional lineage.

Mercedes L. Miller

Mercedes is an internationally recognized speaker, author and consultant whose programs are focused on *Mindset Management: Proven Principles, Practical Application, Profound Results*. The Mindset Management systems and *Create the Life You Desire* programs are used by executives and organizations to increase productivity, drive profits and experience peace in the process. Her words of insight and inspiration can be heard on nationally syndicated radio programs weekly. Mercedes's Executive Consulting, Keynote Speeches or Individualized Training can usher you to rapid results personally and professionally.

For more than 20 years Mercedes L. Miller (pronounced MER-su-dus) has served as a principal consultant in *Mercedes-Empowers, Inc.* providing proven strategies in leadership development, resource procurement, strategic planning and program design. Clients call her the *Master Manifestor*. Mercedes uses her training from Harvard University in Leadership and Economic Development coupled with spiritual insight to guide Executives and entities to greater productivity and higher profits. Leading national seminar houses have contracted Mercedes to share her insights on their public platforms across America. Her efforts have yielded millions of dollars in monetary and in-kind resources for those she serves. She has the keen ability to aide her clients in articulating their desires and then paving the way for the manifestation.

Having trained and keynoted in 49 of the 50 United States, Mercedes has an intrinsic ability to leave an indelible on the hearts and minds of readers and listeners when she speaks and writes. Clients include: Homeland Security, Transportation Security Administration (TSA), Federal Air Marshalls, American Association of Psychiatric Professionals, COMNAVRESFORCOM (International Navy Headquarters), Wake Forest Baptist Medical Center, Winston-Salem State University and more than a dozen colleges and universities.

Mercedes is the author of *Pathways to Peace: Meditations for a Tranquil Life* – a brilliant book on how to use thoughts and words to obtain what you desire and maintain balance in the process. You may have seen her column on *Mindset Management* in your local newspaper as her writings to illuminate the power of the mind have been published throughout the United States and Europe. Ms. Miller's program design for training, outreach initiatives and project implementation work have allowed her entrance into the United Nations and garnered the opportunity to work with more than 61 jurisdictions within and outside of the United States.

Throughout the years she has made an acute impact on national and local organizations. Among her community work, Mercedes served on the *Wake Forest University Divinity School Board of Visitors*. The work she does within the community has caused her to win numerous leadership and community services awards from such organizations as the YWCA and National Women of Achievement

She has been lauded for her volunteer work in the prison system and with women transitioning back into society. Indeed, her work with local, national and international entities makes a difference in the lives of individuals and society as a whole.

To schedule a personal consultation to discuss your needs, contact Mercedes at 336-652-2772 or mercedesleamiller@gmail.com.

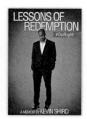

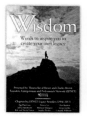

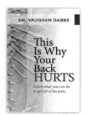

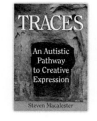

Your

Book

Here

www.PerfectPublishing.com